T0195945

The Snowflake Story

GABRIELLA GRACE

WestBow Press books may be ordered through booksellers or by contacting:

WestBow Press
A Division of Thomas Nelson & Zondervan
1663 Liberty Drive
Bloomington, IN 47403
www.westbowpress.com
844-714-3454

Scripture taken from the King James Version of the Bible.

ISBN: 978-1-6642-4641-6 (sc)
ISBN: 978-1-6642-6823-4 (hc)
ISBN: 978-1-6642-4642-3 (e)

Library of Congress Control Number: 2021920946

Print information available on the last page.

WestBow Press rev. date: 02/14/2024

WESTBOW
PRESS®
A DIVISION OF THOMAS NELSON
& ZONDERVAN

Dedication

To the teacher whose unfailing acceptance gave me the freedom to write, and the courage to express what was locked inside my heart. Thank you for believing that I could, and for knowing what I couldn't see – the threads of a redemptive story were being woven from dark layers of pain.

For my Poppa God, Who continues to fight for me when I can't fight for myself. You are my Strength, my Shelter, and my Only Hope. Thank You for placing such value on my life that You would go to the ends of this earth on a cross, to show me how much I matter to You! As I trust the truth in that sacrifice, help me live it out abundantly as a courageous steward of who You created and intended me to be…uniquely Yours – defined by You alone! You are the One I love.

And for all those who understand the suffocating, black pit of hopelessness and despair. This is for you.

It was in the winter of the year, and my heart
was also in that bleak season. Outside it was cold
and dark, reflecting the same chill and heaviness
that had taken up residence in my soul.

A vision of sparkling white snowflakes drifting softly to earth beckoned me. Restlessly struggling to mirror what I was feeling, I picked up a handful of paper and set my emotions to work.

Fold a sheet in half… Then fold it in half again…Find the exact third of my paper, and line it up to press firmly in a long triangle from the point upwards. Mindless repetition… Fold, and crease. Fold, and crease.

Holding a pure, clean folded triangle, I reached for a pair of scissors and sliced into the unmarred top, whacking off the end at a sharp angle. Talking to myself, I recut that same edge, taking out a large, jagged chunk. "Just like my life," I muttered sadly. "Before I even had the chance to remain unscathed, a huge gash was ripped out of my heart, leaving a hole that has never healed."

As my hands moved, my thoughts churned. "Is this all there is to life? Just the meaningless activity of going through the motions of surviving one more day? Where are the purpose and the value, the meaning of life?"

"And that," I guided my shears into the side of my paper, "has caused so many tears." I curved around to create a teardrop, and 6 tiny paper tears fell to the floor. I watched them go and whispered brokenly, "I'm still crying." The symbol of my liquid pain, a second teardrop joined the first on the other side, as more little tears fluttered down.

"There have been so many thorns along the way, Poppa." I found my words were turning into prayers of not understanding, as sharp, prickly points were carved out of the paper. "And, oh, the thorns have hurt so bad...wounded so deep."

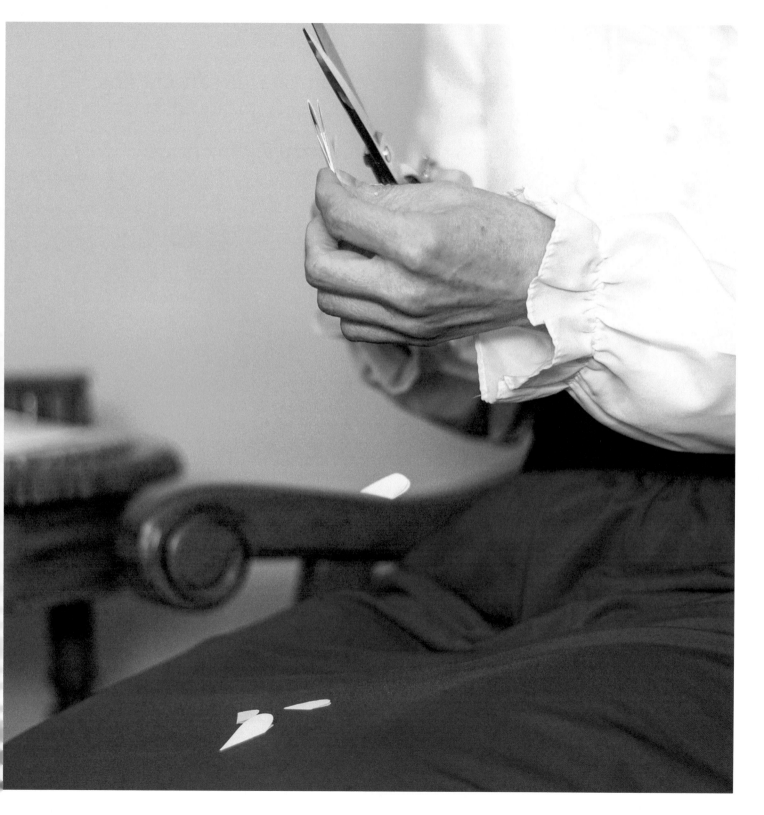

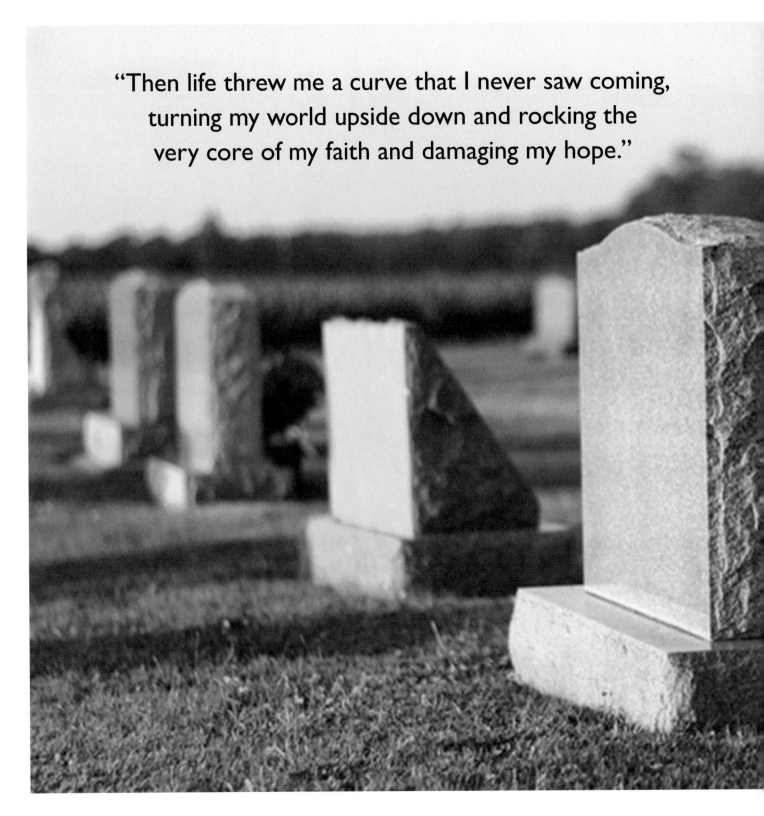

"Then life threw me a curve that I never saw coming, turning my world upside down and rocking the very core of my faith and damaging my hope."

A wicked curve that made no sense whatsoever.
"Lord God, do You even hear my grief?"

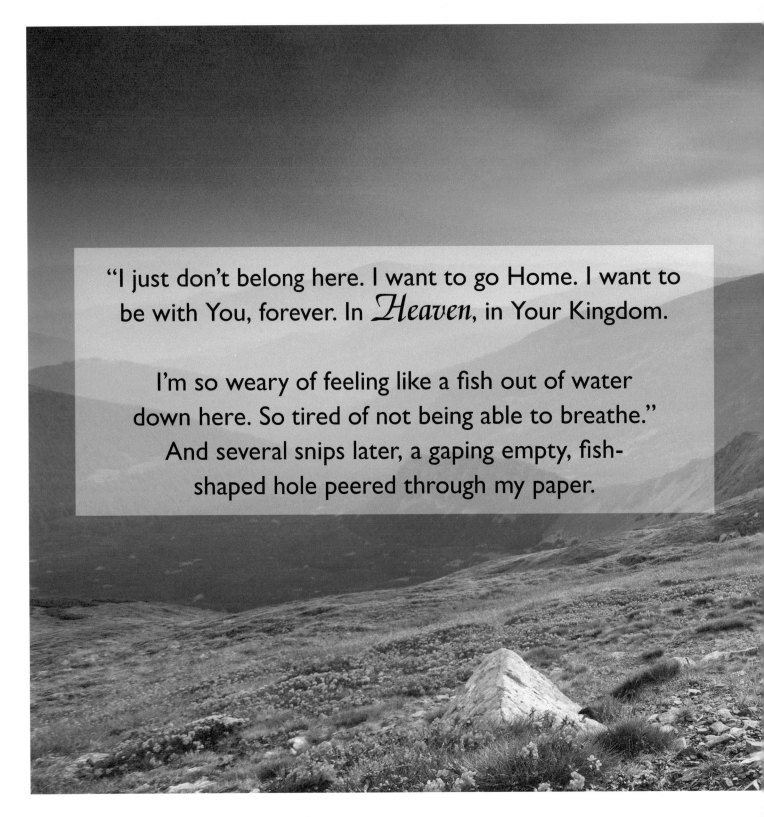

"I just don't belong here. I want to go Home. I want to be with You, forever. In *Heaven*, in Your Kingdom.

I'm so weary of feeling like a fish out of water down here. So tired of not being able to breathe." And several snips later, a gaping empty, fish-shaped hole peered through my paper.

"There's been one dart after the other, Father." I sobbed as I cut slashes into any available spaces. "And when there was finally almost nothing left of me, even my footing was severed in one sharp blow." The pointed tip flew off as blades met paper.

And I was left holding a mutilated, fragmented, destroyed bit of white with no beauty remaining. No rhyme or reason in what had started out as an unscarred, whole, spotless piece of paper. Now it was ruined beyond repair. The story of my pathetic life... the parallel hurt.

The age-old cry of "My God, My God, why hast Thou forsaken me??" echoed through the room as I lay my scissors down. I wept as the wounds inside me crept to the surface and overflowed like a dam that had broken…

Trembling with emotion, I unfolded my pitiful mite of a snowflake; and gasped. Blinking to clear my vision, I stared in disbelief at God's message written in a personal language that pierced through all the layers of the years of pent-up pain and anguish. Where I had seen only the tiniest fragment of my life, God saw the whole picture all along. And as I viewed a complete, exquisite snowflake, He was giving me a glimpse through His eyes.

The "chunk" I had been cruelly robbed of added dimension and character to the entire edge, creating a softened, gentle effect around the circle.

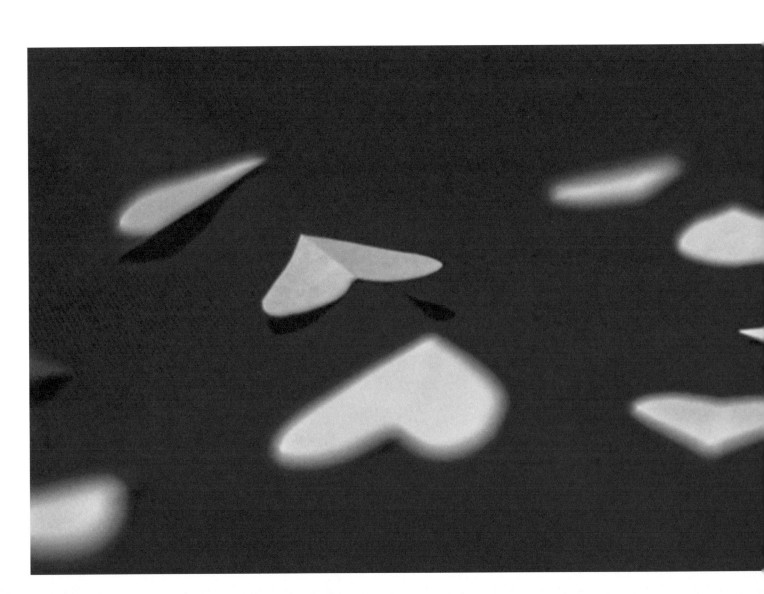

My tears were perfect hearts; portraying the awesome power of a God who shaped them into a new thing, ultimately transforming them into love itself. And, in reality, it was love that first caused those tears to form –

We only cry because we love.

The thorns had become true diamonds: Gems in the hands of the Master Potter with the potential to reflect His light and shine for His glory in a dark world.

That wicked curve was now a graceful dove.
The symbol of that elusive rest all hearts long
for – genuine peace in every storm.

The symbol of Christians everywhere, a fish, now appeared as three connected strands. A threefold cord not quickly broken… I saw in it, "Trinity;" Father, Son, and Holy Spirit.

Every little dart and arrow tip, the stabs and slashes, and marks, lent their own delicate beauty to sweetly enhance and highlight the diamonds and hearts in the big picture.

And the crucial tip, the footing so ruthlessly severed,
stretched out its points in a glorious shining star.
Not a cut had been wasted. And none of it was a
mistake. He used all of it to help me focus upward,
and to bring me close to Him. The truth was that as
His child, my King was only visible when "I" was cut
away, so He could shine in me and through me.

Created on purpose, for a purpose.

And, as I knelt amidst the tears and thorns
scattered across the floor, I bowed my head
in humble grateful worship, and cried,

"Holy, Holy, Holy."

I will praise forever

*"the One Who is,
and Who was,
and Who is to come,
the Almighty!"*

And His words resounded
in the corridors of my heart as

*Jesus spoke in a voice that
spanned time and all eternity.*

"The Spirit of the Lord God is upon Me; because the Lord hath anointed Me

To preach good tidings unto the meek;

He hath sent Me to bind up the brokenhearted,

to proclaim liberty to the captives,

and the opening of the prison
to them that are bound;

to proclaim the acceptable
year of the Lord,

and the day of vengeance
of our God;

to comfort all that mourn;

To appoint unto them
beauty for ashes,

the oil of
joy
for mourning,

the garment of praise
for the spirit of heaviness;

that they might be called
trees of righteousness,

the planted of the Lord,

that He might be
glorified!"

Isaiah 61:1-3

A personal note from the author's heart to my dear readers:

A decade ago when this true story was born, I came to the conclusion that God has a sense of humor…I don't even like snow. In fact, forgive my honesty, but I hate winter with a passion. I've tried to find joy and beauty in it, invariably discovering yet again it is a miserably cold, depressingly dark season. So I simply live with it, enjoying the tiny pieces I am able to; and look forward to the day when my side of Heaven will have dazzling white snow — that is warm ☺ — and knowing eventually spring will always come again here. How like our God, to take what I despise and turn it into something that heals me, if I let Him!

Originally, I had intended to publish this book primarily for adults. (And if you are in that category, God bless you and keep reading, because its message is for everybody!) Then I realized how much I wanted it to reach children too; and with it being done in a simpler format, little ones could totally get it…But I could choose only one genre; and I sensed God calling me to specifically target a sometimes neglected population — the adolescents and college students of today — a confused, vulnerable, desperately hurting people. As I reflected on my own childhood and teenage years, a story like this would've absolutely meant the world to me. Perhaps even altered the course of my life — and changed history! ☺ Just joking on the latter!

Seriously, living life can be hard; horrendously hard as I can testify from my personal journey. Sometimes it helps a bit for someone to meet you in that place and empathize with you in your agony. So this, my brave friend, is for you: I am so sad for the deep wounds and the pain you are experiencing — however old those scars may be. I am genuinely sorry, and if you were here with me, I would wrap my arms around you and hold you close as you weep…So consider yourself compassionately and warmly hugged, and hear this: I wish I could reassure you it will get better now, and be easier. But that may not be true. It will continue to hurt, but perhaps in a less intense, more purposeful way. Because we believers have been given something priceless to hang on to — a visual snowflake promise that in the end, every painful thing will be transformed — even if it takes until eternity! Can you allow that truth to give you a glimmer of hope?? To hold on a little longer; to breathe a little deeper; to draw a little closer; and to love a little harder? Please, please don't give up — for it is always darkest just before the dawn. I am right here with you, for regardless of my desire to tell you otherwise, I am still in the struggle also. We are in this together; but more importantly, God has never left your side. Remember that our feelings can lie, so even when you can't feel His presence, He is there. He is still "El Roi" — the God Who sees — you. And all you're going through. To the core of your soul! He not only hears your silent screams, He cares about you…This wasn't His plan, you know; He created us for an intimate relationship with Him in a purely perfect world. Then the enemy attempted to destroy all of that — but God (don't you love that phrase!) will never be defeated! He gave His Son to pay the price for all our sins, and if we ask His forgiveness and invite Him into our hearts, He will save us. Forever! "Saviour" literally means that…to save His people from their sins.

Thank you so much for joining me and staying with me to the end of this little book. The fact that you have done so tells me how closely you are acquainted with grief, pain, and all manner of abuses. Again, I am so sorry; and if you find yourself wanting to share your story with a human someone who cares, please write me at gabriellagrace147@gmail.com. I cannot fix anything or anyone, but by His grace, I would be honored to listen, and point you toward the One Who is able…for He Who began a good work in you, will not stop till that is completed!

Take courage, dear friend, and let me whisper a parting encouraging word in your ear… It has taken decades but I finally have days where I am enveloped in a cocoon of peace by "Jehovah Rapha" the God Who heals! I cling to Psalm 147:3 "He heals the brokenhearted and binds up their wounds." It doesn't typically happen overnight, but there is peace available in the very middle of the storm…You are so valued. So precious. So wanted. God absolutely loves you — with an everlasting love!

Now, go cut a snowflake, my treasured friend! Let's cover the ugliness in this world with hope and beauty — one snowflake at a time!

Because of Him!
Gabriella Grace

Printed in the United States
by Baker & Taylor Publisher Services